LEGION

THE WESLEYAN POETRY PROGRAM: VOLUME 65

Legion
Civic
Choruses

By

WILLIAM HARMON

Wesleyan University Press

Middletown, Connecticut

Acknowledgement is gratefully made to the following periodicals, in the pages of which parts of this book were first published: *The Antioch Review; Burning Water; The Carolina Quarterly; Folio; The Hiram Poetry Review; kayak; Lillabulero; Mill Mountain Review; Poetry Northwest; Southern Poetry Review; Sumus;* and *transPacific.*

Library of Congress Cataloging in Publication Data
Harmon, William, 1938–
    Legion: civic choruses.

    (The Wesleyan poetry program: v. 65)
    I. Title.
PS3558.A6246L4   811'.5'4   72-11053
ISBN 0-8195-2065-9
ISBN 0-8195-1065-3 (pbk)

Manufactured in the United States of America
First Edition

To my mother
Virginia Pickerel Harmon
and to the memory of my father
William Richard Harmon
(1892–1947)

Contents

LEGION

NOTE

There is in progress a long poem to be called *Looms*, of which *Treasury Holiday* (1970) is the first book.

The choruses paraded here are the middle third of *William Tecumseh Sherman*, the third book of the long poem. They are offered out of sequence, because they have been finished, and they are the right size for a volume. They present, I hope, a coherence that is not necessarily dependent upon their part in *Looms* as a whole.

"Chorus" is no more precise than any other literary word. I have tried to take advantage of its breadth of meaning as regards style, format, and idiom. The "voice" of a given chorus may be—as voices of choruses historically have been—concrete, abstract, or fanciful; and in number it can fall anywhere between the first person plural and the last person singular.

ONE

March: The Mother-Trumpet's Charge Starts the First Trip

We see here drawn up before us now the long rows.

there the stone.
the bronze-bound sea-borne mercenaries of old time there.
there the grand army of the republic aligned & all dead now.
& here our own.
us.

a band of brothers of all things mercy me.

on the tilted green garrison caps see the gold & blood-red piping
    repeat the cocked rat-tat tracks of tracers.
kilts & girls' skirts get lifted ruffled & flourished you see by the same
    wide wind of seeds that prolongs the irregular florid flags.

in the hot air of sousaphonic music as grand & dead as their state Latin
    the mailed mottoes brag maestoso as though nothing had ever
    happened.
empire of paralysis.
motley tubas moo above spit-valves' leakages.

the much-thumbed medals bounce a bit as the leader our director
    administers delivers by downbeat of dumbbell baton the
    wounding coup.
go.
monkey's tail around flagpole the national emblem.
don't tread on snake me.

& snares' split hiss & so now left-footed starts the bugle-horned
    monkey drum major's boot.

The Ceremony of Ignorance

they are burying all the queens this afternoon.
& all the kings & all the emperors the popes the presidents prime
    ministers.

in honor of the long old ceremonies dark clouds have moved over to
    take the sun's place.
the hundred figured flags hang at half staff.

there is no appreciable wind.
the pressure is nearly normal.
no rain to speak of falls the kept pets sleep the limousines are housed
    & few cooks cry.

what can the surviving servants do but stand.
so stand the stony stewards.
hushed butlers' thumbs are lined up by their aprons.
veils screen the housemaids' powdered poker faces.

though wainwrights may be shaken by the wake of death the nurses
    know it as they know their wicked sweethearts.
most mistresses use tissues as they sneeze.

gardeners go to gardens when they die.
the stockpens fall the beasts branded like marked men walk free but
    cannot find their way back home.

The Long Street

Oh wake snakes & walk your chalks.

take a break & look.
self-flags flying in reverse floorboarded back past a dozen wars &
    American manifests.

a man brown-bearded & dressed in a buffalo-plaid lumber-shirt spits a
    sparkling sidewinder of tobacco juice from a buggy seat.
that's real horsehair in back of a real horse.

mercy me God must be a perfectly ordinary individual.
perfectly.

& me mercy me me atomic hailgrains & rat & tat.
worn pieces & flakes breaking down snakewise in a motley cancer cell
    say.

The Reviewing Stand

erect the blue police salute the vehicles.
the black police return the polished loud salute of the wheeling white
    police.

the wounded walk their way from old wars of words & nerves & lilacs.

logistics chokes the tracks with chariots of rhetoric & steel-belted
    appeals to the radial heritage of deathless leather hard as cash.
& revolutionary dedication to tall ideals of the green-crossed palm.

the lip of blood.
the educated knee.
the caught ear deaf as a barber's navel.

polite oil lanolinning easily along.
the polished apple shrugs.
the mixture being much too rich the engine drowns in its own juices
the last lights yellow & brown & die the radio fades.
tat.

now in the patriotic American darkness of deer's knees platoons of
astronauts in native costume defend aluminum penitentiaries
against a million Belgians arguing about language of all things.

the last lilac of napalm politics seeds the wind with metal pollen moles.

the bass drum is the hub of the memorial parade.
& spit-shined in blood-red dresses molten young queens grin.

Echoes from a Procession

It limps the crippled pump.
gold rescued recovered from a cannibalized magnetron dog-skull.

damaged valve weeps much through bandage lagging.

it must be that their metal ears tilt to an indifferent drummer.
for in the kingdom of rhythm detection is obedience.

the man of nightly maintenance advances humming to himself hymns
through the long soliloquies & labyrinths of pipes.
& veins seams lines tubes wires & drainage fields.
peppertrash organization wiring diagrams flow charts batch codes faced
gauges fuse box doors breech blocks circuit breakers transmission
checks & labs of windowed water.

alcohol delivers itself of stillborn smiles.

brooms & wrenches show their bacon teeth.
34 55 89 cleft for me.
sharkhead hammers wake demand breakfast what a racket.
screwdrivers scheme in leather beds.

hunchback transformer hums flat.
do me do me.

bits per second.

needles & anvils index the invisible east.
for lo from there come men & machines riding each other on saddles of
        reciprocal corruption.

& worship.
mutual worship.
the snake that said don't tread on me is dead now.

Dithyramb: Heroics versus Civics

decay descent declension devolution down.

an afternoon with Homer an evening with Wolfgang drawn & ¼ d by
        100 axes.
& now I need a beer.

dream dukes & such mimetic artifacts.
John Wayne's Agamemnon Rex dumb & bloody puffed up & stiff as an
        abandoned boot.
a stuffed shirt inside a brass cuirass 46 extra long.

his eye on the focal woman.
the she.
his sister-in-law twice over.

she who takes her shakeworld titz for a walk on top of what might as
    well be Jericho's Londonderry walls.

for that face that mask of virgin evil the simple eyes that can with one
    quick blank pan shot clip the strings of 1000 life-kites let's cast a
    boy.
just a kid.
with wig & lipstick & pluckbrow.
& sponge jugs kept in place by a sort of Bikejock-built-for-two.

& Odysseus O the man of the many means.
his polymechanic IQ of 80 twice that of any fellow petty king.
a taxi-navigating draft-ducker with his social security number & PENNY
    demotically tattooed across his unwashed forearm.
a wristwatch-busy small-time hive of foolproof watertite longrange
    stratagems designed indeed guaranteed to get us all destroyed.
snake-oil cure-alls big deals party favors bad puns & doubletalk flooding
    his bib.

& for the rest.
mercy me human running boards.
dim guys dumber than any door or night.
a.c.-d.c. football professionals with all the logic of a bag of vacuum
    dust.
sacks.
their Sunday afternoon endures ten years before the golden goalposts
    go.

& that's all folks.
that's the way the last rites was did for Hector the hippodame amen.

decay descent declension devolution down.

slow Homer motion morning news now instant Amadeus replay
    morning sports split Flaubert screen & isolated Moses camera a.m.
    weather.
ah the fugue of fogs rosy with news around its red light's smilings.

The Legion

having been had.
having been screwed blued & tattooed shot at & missed shit at & hit
    used hard & put away wet.
rushed & busted wooed won robbed blind & stood up cold.

having had.
having bitten supper dust & fucked the monkey & nightmared on grey
    trays & marched one one one long light year.
a million miles & blistered backache gutburn bugbite gumboil
    claplimp groincyst armpit boils big as boiled eggs very coarse
    veins & a worn piece.

from being shark'd up to becoming debris d'empire.

mottoes batons standards & piped banners nevertheless & the rat-tat of
    tracers to purfle a dark acre.

we are medieval mariners.
we leave to to to begin to start to kick off the thirty years war.
hundred.

having crossed Poland & the Trojan plain & gone on on our stomachs
    southeast many smoking miles & hit the beach & monkey jungle
    mercy.

for.
for.
what for for what we give up.

eggshell.

eggshell something eggshell funk & panic eggshell self.
eggshell Helen eggshell hell of it.

& what of it.
eggshell shoulder patch & cash-hard laughter takes the cold camp as far
    as getting & forgetting breakfast.

& we say together today whether together or not.

left.
left.

TWO

Sleeping the Present

remembering yestermemory the members sleep the present into
    growths.
teeth-haired mother-dreams who storm night's ocean high wide & ugly
    as an eel's green bleeding gum.

star-parade of fables pale images grow in long rows like toadstools
    gargoyle kernel tumors to be scraped by the long edge of
    language.
the ocean of night's lang-lang-language like an epileptic kleptomaniac
    skimming polyps from the inner skin of pulp & submembrane
    bulbs.

then laid in lines & layers.
lopsided cavalcade of canned scalps.

Addressed to the Department of Municipal Æsthetics

form from morf.
e.g. inasmuch & insofar as formaldehyde exists long underwear exists.

next night the mountain monkey was broken to the plough at last &
    yesterday gave a pint of blood to the Red Cross.
O poor people there was such elation at that.

in another dream I thought I saw Lord Byron flying a milk truck
    backwards look athwart the tender dawn.
dusting crops of sea salt with cut-rate stained glass.

singing a long old song how sorrow is knowledge.

resembling Jack Lemmon he was last seen swimming on a horse or
surfing on a pleated playmate below the neat curved leechcraft
heel of our six-string rainbow.

neuropterous-membraneous arc in the breast-fed northeast of moon
pool & pine-wicker basket of wet mad cats with sprained ankles
turning into polymyositis ache all over.

running horses punctuate an afternoon & running hoses perforate an
afternoon an afternoon like the pocket going bottomless down
into an old pair of pants.

I could swear I saw Charles Dickens in a dream too.

putting in forty hours a day in a cold mind.

a stack of bibles five foot ten skipping supper of gruel & junket just to
dream me back reciprocally.

a Smith brother off the cough-drop box or shortstop for the House of
David.

a retired parachute rigger who moves his hands in his sleep all night.

Addressed to the Department of Municipal Ethics

behold now lo a four-thousand-pound rhinoceros spun spinning around
inside a busy-colored concrete mixer's drum squidded with phallic
lilies.

now sunny side down now up now clockmouth horn gone counter now
aftermath & patted path of mac & mud climbing to the paste sky.

the sky that is that is like a half-hit fly's left wing.

at that kind of angle to the furry fuselage.

& leaking fuel.

say now I think I see Ben Jonson in the shower.
wow he looks like Jackie Gleason an animated bale of whey &
    bazooka's back-blast of furnace breath like so much puppy puke
    in a patent-leather dancing pump.

did you ever see a pump dancing.

Addressed to the Department of Municipal Metaphysics

What Honeythunder the garbageman eats is garbage.
that which he leaves behind on his paper plate uneaten is also garbage.
what he thinks about what he eats is garbage.
the damned paper plate itself is likewise garbage.
the plastic hospital basket with the wax cats in it is synthetic garbage.

the slow fire sermon of the involving public truck he hums hymns
    behind eats garbage & ergo is garbage.
ergo is garbage.
& garbage too the ornate flora that counts the knocking hours.

however he himself is a little lower than the garbage.
but not every quaquaversal thing is garbage.
not the note of every mother-trumpet.

no for there is salt.
there is the gold flow.
there is shooting pool.

Nativities

they the misprints maculate contraceptions horses' mouths lutes lobsters
    tomorrow morning's unborn snow & flukes & flakes of elk-flesh
    eaten 900,000 years ago they're all there somewhere.

this paper's web contains in its manifold matrix of scar tissue some of
the damp pale flat worn piece of bloodtipped toothpick flipped
into a working gutter by one or another.
say Don Juan John Donne Doctor Johnson any John or son.

the bone-fire like a clearance or black sale rockets shot stars of
soot-sparks up into the general breath.
pan-spermia of typical particulates emitted by a civic-minded
kraft-paper factory.

let's hear an ah.

vacant lots junkdumps the contemporary kitchen middens
mayonnaise-white with something modern like a foaming at the
mouth of cleaned teeth.
all in a smoking lather of maggots with a dressing of keen weeds.

yes weeds smells hubcaps weeds foggy cats pasteless tubes loafheels
goats in their hog heaven beerless cans an array of orifices &
meatuses Siamese & multipurpose & heavy-duty.
all held together by what meatpackers are pleased to call binders &
extenders & absolute billions of jelly-gassed cells of romance
murdered & discarded in ill-smelling morning-after diaphragm
fillers from goodbygone nights.
weeds ladies ex-peanuts heads shoulders discordant orchestra of
miscellaneous debris & peas & nuts.

playing mercy me our song & a rat & tat.
minutes of the next meeting seconded motions they're all there
somewhere.

unfused energy matter broken bottles melted down for stained glass
foul papers weeds rusted sunsets barbwire mill-ends & remnants
hardy wild onions springing twice a year through last season's
rats' hairpin ribs.
the small neat backbones of moles that passed away in Calvin's
administration.
Einstein's first bedspread a crazyhazard hapquilt they're all there they're
all somewhere.

upwind of any vacant afternoon or childbirth or dog's ear or pair of
pants.

The Ceremony of Experience

gentlemen expensively dressed in dark colors are making their
statements.
soft words soaked up by the pores of the many absorbent stomachs
constipated monuments sleeves & blotters in Washington.

these statements of surrealpolitik are prepared like coffee in
air-conditioned suites of offices.
reproduced by secretaries who step neat from airline deodorant
advertisements with minds like armpits smooth as barbered
marble.
slick like the pp. of sophisticated periodicals that say compleat & kudos.

duplicated collated distributed & issued to the pool of cupped coppery
palms held out by the mercy me professional press.
the journalists that style themselves the fourth estate.
that is to say the praedial residuum of uliginous turpiloquence etiolated
under the glacial cyclops pyramid of lords temporal lords spiritual
& the grogram broad-based commons.

these foot-long hot-dog mental midgets queue up at the world-sow's
       hindmost tit that bitter end pink puckered faucet with the wrinkled
       rubric UNCLE.

now these are the precincts of supreme moral law.
sawn stones laid down to die between Virginia & Maryland names that
       do honor to queens of England from the sixteenth century domini.
manly women dressed in dark who issued tough prepared statements
       too.

The Ceremon(y)(ies) of Mutability

the road to hell is paved with theologians.
the golden gates are hanging on their hinges weeping.

an orphaned wildebeest stares at the ruined altar rinsed in the
       Sunday-funny Dutch reformed light.
a hundred thousand hungover white candles hear an ah.

wicked dirt from pterodactyls drops like preternature's dumb bombs
       'pon the candy-paper mobile homes of us posthistoric men.

Papists & Maoists.
kleagles & kleavers & Amos & Remus & old Adam Bum.

they speak in tongues from limb to limb.

THREE

Muscatel Morning

must be.
let's see.
must be let's see morning.
yes must be.

let's see.
now.
Monday.
yes.

why.
there they go.
my.
first things first.
first things first.
first things first things first things first.

rat.
tat.

thirst.

must be.
let's see let's see.
let's just see now.
August.

August oh hell no not August.
this cold must be February.
so cold must be must be be March.

march.
rah.

so.
man holds bag bag holds bottle bottle holds wine wine holds man.
yes sir.
that's that.
wine man holds.
a circle a held circle as perfect as the pupil in God's one good eye.

one good eye.
one why one because hell without one good eye round as the sweet
twinkling mouth of the pint I mean I mean without that one good
eye well how in hell could he see.

What Is the Question

W hat in the world.
in the spider trees.

& what have I not done for money in my time.

why is the boot wearing a wig.
why in the world & how.

is it a black boot a black wig.
it is & the scalp black as the long-winded hair.

it figures.

but suppose both were not black but blue.
or mauve or mulberry or polyunsaturated red mercy.

mom o' golly a red wig is that possible.
ah what is not.
ah.
the final figures figure fugally.

I smell smoke it is the silk bush yonder or is it.
is it one of the daughters of language.
her breast that burns or burning buttocks socketed.

the road curves dips why.
under today's rainbow curve the road avoids going into the ocean how.
& the world it curves dips avoids to what precise degree what.

to what degree then do deep knee bends follow suite.
is it therefore a question only of up & down.
or of side to side as when combing hair lying down caught in a
        jack-jawed trap.

scar tissue figures the fish in the fishbowl figures I figure it figures.
what in the spider trees the dog grass the egg-blue sky.
& what too of the blood the green the cloud of no color the mother of
        rust.

& finally what of it if it figures.

The News

$\mathcal{\&}$ now the latest from South Dakota.

the boy in blue pulled up a parking meter this morning & used it to beat
        a buffalo to death on the main street of Sioux Falls.
where in the name of heaven the great beast came from is anybody's
        guess.

what was he doing on the wrong side of the street the rampaging
        avalanche of untidy upholstery with unspeakable liquid mixtures
        dripping from his black ripped lips.
& the world wonders about that yawing cue.
could it actually have been a penis.

so merciful heaven.
thank you thank you for cops whose winged shields have not yet
        deprived them of the blessed presence of mind to reach for the
        nearest bludgeon cudgel or even parking meter with twelve full
        minutes still left on it & brain that that that.
unmannered beast.
because who knows one may now & again see fit to take off down the
        main street of Sioux Falls or someplace else why who can say.
mercy me it's anybody's guess.

the confrontation episode took place happened between the morning
        rush & the lunch hour that slackish time when police officers
        ordinarily relax.
so Sioux Falls can count itself lucky.
one man was on his toes alert.

for otherwise.
otherwise that unprepossessing creature would could have turned china
        shops literally.
scenes of unexampled carnage friends & neighbors blasted corner store
        plate glass into supernovae butterflies snapdragons underinsured
        maidenheads God-jammed radio stations haywire warfare &
        anything & everything that can go going.
all out O.

heavy-duty anvils dropped into dishpans & turds berserk in cut-glass
        punchbowls.
amok undignified foreign-looking unhousebroken plus toting on top of
        it all a shifting old hump of saturated fat & gristle.

Editorial Commentary

the verso of the nickel now shows Monticello.
a structure humped somewhat like a buffalo.

but hardly ha hardly the kind of entity to go tearing unshod mind you
      unshod down the chartered pavement of downtown Sioux Falls.

Monticello keeps its broad mouth shut.
like somebody who's given birth to a fire & so knows how it burns.

Taps & Coda

O.
tempora mores God & Montreal.

empire going out of biz must sell lost our cherry lost our principles.

blue blizzards of lost leases & skirmishes the ticktape alleying up in
      cyclone's stock of suck & vacuum holy Moses.
out of mind & business empire relinquishes its one load the ignorant
      generals quack & snarl in idiomatic mastiffese.

tilt the machine until it registers TILT & lights go out.
your only buffalo nickel swallowed whole & gone.

bloodlover emperor loses grip the genes & seminal esemplasm elope to
      atmosphere atoms rainflakes flagstones mercy me the street is
      nervous.
chamber of deputies up in motley smog the glad glass ads of mad ave.

Ignatius Loyola releases a prepared statement that states that we ought
      to minify the middleman by drowning our livestock in our sewers
      directly.
at that the septic men & the pig-grinders flood the house of scoundrels
      with a cubic acre of lobby dough.

it's time makes the matrix of mortality & me.

ah well just like a political machine or anything else on What's-His-
      Name's green earth a poem's a mouth at one end & a rhythm
      at the other.

ahem testing testing one two one two huff puff.

in recent developments on the hill the pork-workers' international
      brotherhood's head hood has demanded time-&-a-half for double
      space.
their spokesman spoke.
U huvu un umpurtunt unnuncumunt uf gruut unturust tu thu nutuun.

see see Memphis under a thousand fathoms of tobacco juice.

buffalo's brain the half cantaloupe you'd expect even the seeds neatly in
      place & all all asleep.
shaped like the newborn ponies seahorses will deliver.

dragonshrimp beewolves bear & buffalo down from the royal mountain
      of earth with too much momentum tum-tum-tum.
your house down.

Curriculum Mortis

Pounded pounded pounded on the nuthouse door.
fist reduced to blood fingernails coming undone assaulting the iron hide
    with jabs hooks chops & uppercuts.
bones in the hand just so much loose ice in an icebag hanging at arm's
    end.
& O the nuts manned the barred windows with their craze-crazed eyes.

bones showing white through the busted knuckles broke the front door
    down.
then a dead light at an inner door.
what's the matter.
let me in.
what's wrong.
it was Dad bought a Picasso sixty thousand bucks took saw & scissors
    he cut it up Mother & Child a puzzle in pieces let me in.
no now you better go away.
shaggy worn pieces mercy no let me in.
no go.
please let let me let me in.
go away.
no.
go.

so pounded pounded on the great gate of the federal pen with a
    ballpeen hammer.
heavy head flying off the handle toward the cons at their checked
    windows with moon-mean eyes of stir.

it was Monopoly gave Park Place for Waterworks little green houses &
    big red hotels chance & charity & jeopardy & dice & jail & ruin
    aplenty.

& at the nunnery pounded on the door swinging a sword.
& O the stitched virgins the sisters bridally prim in pious bifocals
     averted from the leaded windows & glad gold of a gone throne
     restored.

was slot machinery bulging pregnant & laboring my way with jolly
     doses of silver dollars a veritable cherry orchard & plums too &
     brazen bells & watermelons & local specials.

& lemons.
you know the land.
lemons equal nothing nothing nothing in that land.

& at last of course at the ribbed gates of the graveyard pushed.
it's fingers of tongue & prick that excavate those holes so the warm
     worms' cold old work can go on continuing.
-uum.

& O the hired diggers with eyes so deep & dirty dark forevermore.
& he fell through the hole to hell that hath no doore.

Cheap Sleep

lockers lockers lockers lockers.

yesteryear highschool lockers.
as though someone hungry were fishing for us through the painted
     dented sheet metal.
leaden in effect if not lead really & scratched with nasty things.

doors louvered with smell of physical education shoes & devilled egg.
the racks the long old rows of hooks the hall America
     my motherfatherland.

blunt hooks baited with hats.

salty sweatbands perforated to let light through.

shoes shoes & shoes shoes abed their laced & grommeted jock eyes my
    eyes too.

Stores

general merchandise the old testament.

wares notions sundries dry goods ready to wear candy hats cash & carry
    Harry Truman making change thanks.

cut-rate kickshaws ten cents each three for a quarter & Jeremiah shifts
    to turn his burnt eyes from the living zenith to our grain elevator
    temple of the wounded the dead.

poor people.

general rank & file matrix of merchandise womb of goods left left left
    right left.

halt.

fallout.

there's Humphrey pumping drugs all out & sundae soda cracker pop
    sip water phosphate wax straws wrapped in yesterday's news
    today's olds forgot & never brought to mind or not.

taurorrhea over thanaturf & coffeegrounds rabbit tobacco Black Maria
    sold to American a wide sidewalk of good intentions.

we make no compromise with kwality.

hey hey sleeves for sale clearance on cuffs happy hour's here our whole
    day-old stock of handles reduced from discount for quick sale dead
    end remaindering bonus for buttons marked down shark'd up
    mark offs cash & carry dry debris register laid away & bad goods
    hard wares debacle soft sale we do not deliver in God any longer.

lost our let me pray discipline.

modesty.

sorry chandlers & economy amen.

Sam Grant making change John Newton selling slaves wholesale retail
on consignment Sherman hero with a purchase order signed &
countersigned for cavalry mounts thirty-six per cent off buy pay
now later soon joy.

tonite only lad-o-rama let us pray order exercise good food night sleep
green leafy punctuality red rich meaning amen making change
back.

come to the world of wheels & deal deal deal with the deal king himself
you might whip our potatoes buddy but you can't beat our meat.

home-made key lime pie me to pray thanks for the soup you amen
January inventory check Adam check Sheth check Enosh check
$million in freezedried shrimp in warehouse chillbox on the way
to Mars orbit check.

kwik things on a stick check chocolate drops on paper strips oh yes eat
it all & make change backwards much obliged ma'am amen
brother unhand that candy jar.

a profit's not without honor.

then when will Ipana of yore rise from the new testament of the dead
or Mounds & Cords of old.

out to lunch be back one-thirty eat eat kids free it's bat day booths for
ladies.

thank you call again making general change pray lay in the lap of Him
our merchandise America.

ka.

The Path to the Porch Being Paved

On honk of horn another uncle's horse knuckles under.
another aunt's apron loses flowers in the machine of rain.

The House in the River Valley

beyond the bank looms a dam.
back of the dam a mountain.

clouds on beyond.
a darker grey there.
then stars then wards of darkness a different paradise.

modern commerce employs a romance tongue.
FIDELITY FEDERAL PRESERVES ITS CUSTOMERS.
you see a billboard cartoon it shows you Mr. Average Man inside a
      closed sealed canning jar smiling.

the bank is dark under the stars after dinner.
the cartoon is lighted the dam is illuminated by powerful flood lights.
the mountain & clouds are gone.

electricity travels through miles of wire hysterical.

we are scared to put our money in the mattress.
we are scared to send our children to the schools.
we are scared to drop our letters in the mailbox.
we are scared to stick our fingers in the sockets.

FOUR

Everyone Eating at Once

Swordfish steaks cut the cooked water.
personal as sleep.

herds herds oh how many a head of.
beeves burn in back yards.

mercury passes the soft crack.

green pears appear in the suburbs.
they have been specially wrapped in translucent tissue.
paper labels hasten to paste their selves to lanolin bananas as mottoes
      grow on station-wagon bumpers.

now flowers doze in the lapel of the afternoon the sky a cry of chrome.
the hard crack line is crossed.
the exclusive box for artichokes from California skates generously into
      the Judas of fire.

personal as sleep.
veal cutlets speak & bacon oinks in the circle of ore.

Annals of Bondage

eating fins.
living on buttes.

rusted sunset over shadow cabinet.

but nothing new is as new as a new tennis ball.

twist of the slotted key that engages the started tongue of tin that lets
the breath in with a split hiss.

three shook balls are born into your palm like bleach-white baby chicks
marked with bold black symbols.

& by the same token ha nothing dead is as dead as a dead tennis ball.

all you know grey & bald & sour to the nose.

abandoned or lost in the most remote veteran closet between a vacant
mousetrap & a Blue Goose shoebox so.

so very very dead indeed that even if dropped plumb in a perfect
vacuum from forty stories up it would not on impact with the
solid sidewalk bounce one single solitary inch.

no sir.

yet we keep the key & spiral strip of separated tin & keep too our
deadest balls in their original cylindrical containers refusing to do
away with them or let them once lost stay so.

or consign them to the gnawing of the ignorant dog or dew no we keep
everything.

party favors opera menus platform planks empty pens expired
guarantees mildewed report cards home-made Valentines gone to
gangrene Negroid negatives threadless spools exhausted jelly jars
bulk ads that dent the mailman's back played games cancelled
stamps Monopoly money worked puzzles parted laces solved
problems penetrated mysteries hairnets limericks & keepsake
heirlooms.

alas.

used up Nashes tarnished awards for running up mother-of-pearl
pen-knives topheavy tops dime teeth calling cards grounds corks
caps bulbs butts stubs bits.

debris d'empire shark'd up & never been discharged.

now our butte overlooks the great plain.

flat all the way to the straight hard-edged horizon line in the all-yellow
     precincts west & south of us.

broken if broken at all only by a single dark fin crossing the aforesaid
     sunset.

Ifs & Cans

Continued from last month i.e. December 9378 B.C. old style.

cans.

cans of soup cans of silver & wheat cans of women real Second
     Corinthians in cans of February beer & feet.

scalps eggs & laughter & I American say cans not tins but cans.

everymanjack learns with mother's birthday milk that the cans are not
     tin.

not tin okay but if not tin then what.

then what you say then merciful heavens mercy me emerald platinum
     mink.

emerald can for green beans platinum for artichoke hearts or mock
     turtle wings.

mink for tennis balls for ball bearings from the Perfect Circle people
     the Beaker people & their high-heeled gotterfunken cleft for me.

send to the Stanneries for cans for imaginary gardens with real turds in
     them.

no but back to cans of women now if not tin for them then what.

then this.

hermetic di-methyl-oxy-Desdemona.

& spurge purgeth thin phlegm vehemently.

how's that.
or this.
cut-rate misericordia carbon steel rolled sheeted stamped & cut with a
     rat & a tat & a that is a that.

but but but.
asks Thomas the saint most human his indexfingerprint a
     counterclockspring of ticking 'sblood.
but how do they get the woman into the can.

but.
how.
but how my God my good man canneries are operated twenty-four
     hours a day to put sardines into cans for you but the sardines are
     herring & the tin is steel & you.
old funny-looking old you you ask how.

so I say unto thee Thomas I say emerald platinum mink orchid whole
     deal dovetailed dado the Elephantine Papyrus eagle lion & last &
     least least the cerebrations of stellar Kant the Alexanderissimus of
     metaphysics.
conquered the whole known world & died one of those sad & early
     deaths never having had the the the time to ask how.
how they get the woman into the can.

imagine asking Aristotle a thing like that.
ah honored doctor ahem how do they so & so sir.

they just do.

Shadow Cabinet

the tongue in its deep kitchen cooks things too.

such numbers as dragons burglars characters.
they pitch sharp active shadows in the pantry of bone behind blind eyes
      a-dreaming.

iron tar & dark leaf in the cast dark.

EAT.
eat.
EAT.
eat.

edges angles a hundred crowded sorts of grey.
also a hundred dollars' worth of ordered flowers around the day's dead
      in his one polished one-time box.

eat at the terminal cafe EAT.
eat to a nice Seth Thomas metronome.

EAT.

sleep though seems to be the creature's normal state.
with the waking world only a lady in waiting & all the great chain gang
      of being there simply to make good solid sleep possible.

the bald O speechless baby neonatus deodatus.
baby sleeps dreaming endlessly O O endlessly dreaming sleeps baby.
each full-size new blue eye being exercised independently.

Four Men

low & inside.
he walked him.

in your body the nameless bones.

a swing & a miss.
strike three.

the nameless bones in my body.

some you win some you lose & some the good old Lord rains out.

to second & over to first.
in time.
a double play.
no hits no runs no errors.
nobody left.

nameless bones in everybody's body.

FIVE

How Need & Death Are Balanced on a Blade

the clock chews her own offspring note by note.
her litter.
for motes of music float in the sunset light so sadly.

how old is such sunshine how old such sad shadows how old how old.

& the slug's unlovely sole deposits a snot-silver trail & writes things
    much uglier than fuck or cunt on garden wall & walkway.

veins & seams of weakness in the rock matrix bristle with mica.

broken bricks more broken broken bricks bottles of old oil in the gone
    corner a can of gas.
a pretty beet-seed envelope folded over inside a shoe with its dry &
    wine-dark oxblood tongue hung out.
this stuff in the hoe-&-shovel shed is shadowed now by the slug's sunset.
untold catalogues of dust-tufted tools the sag & sog of cartons the doll
    cotton the toy town the wooden horse the electric track for
    long-gone locomotives.
those on-loan notes the final figures.

edge-burnt & bourbon-circled an old end table leans against a roll of
    blue linoleum so sadly.
& on it now a '47 hubcap that caps a hub no more but serves instead as
    a bowl for bolts with no nuts deployed at random among dead
    webs.

in the heavy-duty containers of white ice cream canteens of blood are
    buried.
industrial dust & cocker scabs make cartridge belts that ring Saturn in a
    waltzing free-fall jig the final figure the tune the melody of Yankee
    Doodle Don't.

you know I think I would give anything to talk with Bach today.
or Dante.

but what what would could & should I say.

meister I would say maestro I must so sadly say do you speak any
    English.
& the blessed slug passing between us & the rusted sunset has as much
    to say.
he is like us all in that he says as much as he must & no more or not too
    much more.

the death wish is the law of gravity.
the motes of music float through the filtered moonrise light.

Lumber

 now is it not an ordinary paradox.

to hear from afar the steady heavy strokes with the alternate steady light
    ticks tailing offbeat after in the international rain that solves the
    kingdom of knots under the tongue.
but not once in the fugue of forest fogs to catch sight of the bright
    heads.
like lightninglight.

the heads of many axes of laughter falling & as they fall felling.

Diapason: Bodies of Water

données unknowns morse seraphim abortions all.
all go in rain down drainpipes & up pipes as smoke in the form of fog
the grand clouds welcome with a big hel-lo.

what's not the fire's very self is darkness gnarled in looping shadows
scooped in twice-reflected scar-tissue light.
pollution creates a mixed atmosphere conducive to splendid sunsets.

rainy day & sunny day go away.
do anyway.

& that is that & a day & a day & data unmistakable givens & may be a
maybe.

predicamental meditations entered into by the millions upon millions of
millions among our miscellaneous vicissitudes.
nuisances offspring strokes of luck & genius rays of light & lines of rain
together today.
the jail of rain the blood the green the mercy me words of confidence &
folly.

like home permanent.
it's not home God knows & God knows it's not permanent but she
does it.

hey.
the hottest item on the best-buy list this week is AMERICAN METAL
CLIMAX.
call your broker.

heterogeneous splendors over even Chicago in the two twilights under
industrial dust under pollution like burnt oil spreading its
spectrum of signatures as rainbows across pressed tar or mist of
blisters.

the curb & gutter of such scenery the local color of lo-cal nightmares
    only.
these three or four peculiar greens no sunlight through a leaf could
    generate.

& every every every human nerve a hive hissing.

hell.
answer the going on & off of day & day in & out with new teeth dying
    to the wide wind & bald to the bucking light & deaf.
        deaf to the self-centered gull who doesn't know himself from a
        hole in the water.

Solo Epistolary Chorus: Infirmity & Theology

here & now.
dear doctor colon.

it lamely leaks this aching sore wounds thought & cripples up sleep.
wryjawed up the steep-spined stepped spikes of a a a stone-stiff neck
    the snapshot-window of our dearest door the door to sleep is shut
    by frost & fog now.

lo look idiosyncratic crystals circumcumulate into a miniature
    chandelier for the ballroom of my lower abdomen lo.
I hope to hell it smells to high heaven for I want God to know.

the existing key to things as is is a misfit.
but my mind meanders.

well now there.
our induration has begun to thaw & I think it looks like we've got that
    suppuration licked & the desquamation's scaling down very nicely
    & I can almost all but walk.
hey doc put me on a poster for St. Jude's day.
get me a new tooth.
appoint me to the chair of sp-sp-sp.
speech.

therapy.

I I well I just wonder why you hoard so many towels swabs & sponges
    in this constant gore booth the scream-permeated-curtained
    emergency kraal.
pyramidal hierarchies of towels on trays capture the flicking tail of my.
eye & don't think for a second I didn't for a second see that dead old
    lady down the ha hall.

as now wow you doctor dug digged my person's deepest-seated pus up
    in ingots from their divot-pocked pockets I called on God until at
    last as I copped a grip on the sweating table-pipes the hammock
    slacked & when you frowned down into my prep-scraped groin
    crotch I grinned giggled.
your killpain xylocaine is an oily & transparent lie the stinkish hurt is
    still killing.
me.

again I call on God O the words go up enough enough but all my
    imperfections must be being on my infected head at once all
    dancing on that has-been pin.
for mornings between mirror & egg I palpably balden.
mercy.
new moles appear for people to interpret.
item a Gemini whose moon's in Scorpio has a reversed big dipper on
    his left forearm.

so O.
O say scab-petalled alto-throated flower-mouth of me something.
something heavy with depth hanging on a glade of brass.
hypostatic pith of lesion.
is it perfume from a dressing that begets this grim digressing.

well now there.
the white towel lies deflowered limply folded on the grey tray.
a ubiloquent young tuning fork demurely tunes all the halls &
      corridors just before a woman robot's unadenoidal voice names
      names.
I think she has my number.

the things the instruments are laid out fang-fearful for the
      nerve-emergency.
the nurse's personality is Coolidge's restillborn mercy me ma.
hic est porcus.
see see where my blood streams in the fundament.
O negative O.

the death wish is the law of gravity.
aromatic gravity pulls the matched twin balls down toward the center
      of the hurting earth & there the midwife death wish welcomes
      them hel-lo.
on his iron horns' tips' own proper points.

the sane sun is a pig eating a snake me & bougie the burglar breaks &
      enters me me.
me mercy.
so God damn so may the mad moon's hoof crease-clip your capped
      head with hooks with scaling tools & crescent wrenches crawling
      percolated parasiting nightmares of klaxon-klieging spot-lit
      malpractice.

you leech-bled Washington you leech-bled Byron & now're
    leech-bleeding me me O doctor Hippocrates incarnadined in tooth
    & bill with blood of my blue-shielded blood & of my flesh flesh.

insanity my ass identity crisis hell.
& even chronic cureless epidemic tee-terminal
    polyhyperdiplomegametateragigaschizo*para*paranoia   doubled   &
    redoubled in razor-sharp spades when vulnerable that's easy that's
    nothing that I can take.
what I can't stand God & good my doctor is these real steel knives &
    wicks literally exercised in the secret precincts of my physical
    person's flesh.
not the symbolic but the actual.
ache.

I guess I owe a cock too.
okay so I owe.

I owe a cock & hang hereby my hernias in your weeping tree sincerely.

Taking a Rubbing

the pen diddles the pad & gets diddled back.
like like.
worn piece a worn piece as a dry stick for fire of dry sticks.

or an epic dichter in the saddle bucked & bucking.

there is a man O. Felix Culp whose wife's named Lucy Sue.
they flog the floor from noon to noon & say they always do.

worn saddle sore on a worn horse back.

his dark girl is named Phyllis so for short he calls her Phyl.
they scale the sky from time to time & think they ever will.

will O will O windy will thy work is hell on we weak willies.

or.

or.

or is it Suzy Lou.

Triple Hymn

(Irregular, with irregular refrain)

Uncle Sam's my usual muse but.
Calliope Urania & radioactive Polyhymnia attend for now noctes atque
     dies patet the door & yonic yawn.

under under the town & down down in the dingled dark where dirt
     lurks doubling its unlovely half-life minutemeal.
there nowanights in a hundred neon shoes the undifferentiated id
     endures.
it the id das Es is does whatever it is that it does & whatever it does it
     does all the time & does it what's more on one one-note note.

f.

wakes & works without sleep or wakeless sleeps a-dreaming.
a floorboarded tuning-fork f to which one need not palm explicit
     allegiance.

our home hole is there da there the unzoned mildewed classic wilderness
    the desert featured conspicuously in all the great scriptures of
    antiquity.
since the dumb dim id is all back its back is always turned so that the
    old words down there fuckuckuck each other's medusa kilokuntz
    with arson prix.

the twice-tolled tropic of excrement where love's strafed tent leans in
    the steady wide wind of will & blind pain in the jail of ringing
    rain rain.
the seedy birth the windy birth gapes like an open glove compartment.
a steady wind because it turns to stone when it disdains to turn at all.

oil & all ill liquids là the id dam drinks & drops.
the tired & mildew-shirted curb under the rusted sunset is a part-haired
    worn piece O & under the no more virgin moon flowerless whore
    leoparded with cleated footprints & driftwood the hoof-crooked
    signs of inert gas gesticulate hysterically in the one language most
    alien & most remote.

language to the dumb-mute id's id is I'd say the daughter of forgetting
    begotten under the broadcast of the dark dorsal of the
    sponge-soled moon.
the radio says rain the commercials urge listeners to be faithful to the f
    fork for the f fork is a reciprocating engine pump & pump a
    dancing pump.
the word & the moon both daughters of one cosmquake womb matrix
    & sprung alike from the one dark celestial triple cock whose
    coded name they say the marcharcharching band of buxom
    humping stars spells out.

our word's a mother mouse the owl of Uncle Sam will swallow.
& what the owl brings back up again when the undigested sun comes
    up is what the morning's poem resembles as the dance of dogs
    two by two & the moon-dewed wilderness ostensibly dissipates.

however the singular lordly id is an old con so can't be conned so ladies
please breathe your clear & lovely breath collectively through
ours & all our lines & lenses.

Paint

tar.

these the final figures.
Pollocks.

kitchen flotsam backforth a rat-tat tangle of lines scrapping traffic of
figments the wreckage cordage.
make a face.

negotiations navigations round records of fingerprints riddles one & all.

the lands & grooves dance in dancing rings.
catatonic & charlestoning loose the fling & swing singing in moving
square rings.

the dancing fighters whorl.
is life like that.

like cloverleaves of au'mobiles prefiguring faces shaped like pained
blind men kicking black as.

Tell & Tell

in the bathtub.
superfluous white corpuscles' corpses are sloughed off the deadstock
offal in a brine vat boiled to seafoam soft-crack yeast the perfume
the soap.
from sheep's tallow.

pale fat floats dreamily off the practical bone.
rendered down to the fact of the actual matter the marrow of all things.

the varied fats float in lacy galaxies free of the bone the spiked spine &
        core of organic concentration.
sensitivity intensified so & so & so in a few special spots the unqualified
        stars like nipples & petals on a bough.
overhead with six-tipped snow-Saturns the flakes of fire the soot all in
        free fall the bone ash the what is left.

bereft smoke of star & as bonus a fugue of lilac fogs in orbit of rose
        howitzer & shrapnel of all things.

zero gravity the sun & moon never sleep but tell tell & tell tell tell.
tell beads & tell bullets the telling telling told.

<u>SIX</u>

long, too long, O land,
Travelling roads all even and peaceful you learn'd from joys and
*   prosperity only,*
But now, ah now, to learn from crises of anguish, advancing, grappling
*   with direst fate and recoiling not,*
And now to conceive and show to the world what your children
*   en-masse really are,*
(For who except myself has yet conceiv'd what your children en-masse
*   really are?)*

1865

Evangelical Chorus

Soon now I'm going to go to heaven in a hydrogen ballon with
   messages for Daniel & Rebecca B. Boone.

the united states of America are going crazy absolutely loon.
gone soon John Wayne so bloody bloody soon.
vanilla villas upon the moron moon.

A War Rosary

Star.

shell.

Willy Peter for WP white phosphorus falls.

usually an airburst sure for purposes of illumination but against the
      VC we set them see for surface impact to burst & burn.
burn see those hiding in the bushes & whatnot you see & take advantage
      of their superstitious irrational non-Western fear of mutilation of
      all things.
did we teach them a lesson.

The Day

& that was that day.
& that was that.
that day was the old rat & tat day the green canteen of blood put every
      fire to shame.

that day it rained black burning bananas & ears & they froze remember
      into strips of mildewed dandelionhearted white-haired toes of
      dogshit aging on the ground that was glass & growing old.
the flaw of flame then tried to beat the band to eat the glass.
glass because the day before was that remembered day it snowed wow
      a reinforced corporation of bull 'gasms slouching toward
      Bethlehem to be steel.

a day for barefoot space-travel a day for squaredance competition
      finals on & on into the night well mercy me inside the dancing
      blood-red barn O.
& that was that day.

not the day it snowed wisdom no.
& not the day screwed-up courage struck its sticking point & stricken
      got good & stuck in the kleptomaniac Atlantic's windpipe.
God no.

the day the mundane moon shed its maidenhead & bid adieu to its old
      skin & gave up more than one ghost & the day the transparent
      parents' prepared statements & canned goods all went bad & the
      old newspapers misspelled every single word but maggot.
tha2 qaj ms tud.
ahem that day is ah today.

it rains lost toads on tar-dark roads under lo the tread of discipline's
      slick eliminator car it rains decent burials for committees of
      windshield insects.
it rains jails & clipboards of names & numbers from under hubcap mud
      & license-plate imprisonment.

at the end of the straits under the cut-throat sunset there is still the jail
      of seamless radio rain singing singing singing up a storm O.

it is so raining rain you know.
it's raining a strict & liquid diet of days.

that'll be the day buddy & it will.

At the Window

they they shoot the breeze they chew the rag the fat.
they plight their troth & what is that.
they are all alike they are going home now nothing changes.

why here they come again no there they go.
O lord here they come unsure enough they come their merry way as if
      as if as if all the old boarding houses & comic strips were to tip
      over dumping out all the chambers of deputies all the committees
      of the whole all the more perfect unions all the prisoners of war
      & peace the daze of the weak.

they are all alike the shadow cabinets the bare refugees deaf as
      doornails now to all the great languages & forbidden all the
      great meals on O my lowercase lord religious grounds.
now the mouths of the months became mounds.
the rows of empties grow & there they go now mercy me.

no here they come they come to town so God be with you i.e. goodbye.
all's well that ends.
commercial travellers gay deceivers wholesale fugitives punch press
      operators shop stewards rubber drummers sandwich men stick
      men titmen deacons mouthpieces tycoons they are all alike.

the foot-long hot-dog laughs are all alike the manholes are all alike the
      bumpers on the second-hand hearses are all alike & all busy as
      the typical one-eared doorman at the average row of teeth
      graveyard.

they are talking turkey with their forlorn hands.
forlorn.
the weekend smacks its lips for them.

they mail the mail they nail the nail.
women waxing wood.

as they call shots they hear the heart of earth methodically applauding
      as though on a guaranteed annual salary of salt.
of bloods & greens the grand ovation stands.
they are going going gone on home now the runners up the royal
      families the chambermaids the switchboards of snakes the veterans
      of foreign worn pieces the ministry of ink the department of tape
      ta ta.

no O lord here it itself comes now the bureau of bureaucracy so God
      be with you sisters of emptiness brethren of breath cousins of
      silence children of therapy clan of abandon wives of division
      family of disconnectedness.

& the home-long aunts as though on a front porch together swinging
    the aunt of party the aunt of church the aunt of enterprise the
    orphans of orphans.

Hallmark is our novel Time our song.
have forgotten the first three words of Rock of Ages.

anvil-shaped the chorus of wounds motors along among the waters &
    greys of the five-o'clock sky the sky of becoming becoming.
horses' shoulders are our novels the knees of deer our song the organ
    tune of Quaker cartons cleft for me.

we weep the more because we weep in rain.

stars equal pills.
they have destiny without character.
the sky at motley midnight is busy with disputed symbols.
like a felon's palm.
this line see is life this line is love.
you are here.
the interstates are our cathedrals.

but they they have banks under their eyes & branches of plasma under
    their blank nails that grow as slow as courage.
their hair is long words.

it is better to have loved & lost.

now now your head is a dead tongue Lord O John James Charles
    George Thomas Robert Edward & homeless Michael lover of
    heights.
hexameter is six feet in the grave they are all alike & nothing changes.
on the eighth day of a new year their same faces pass the B-52 news
    like a series of teeth.

gone thrones hard cash & symbol toys on the jaundiced chain of
    earth-tolled time.

another bomber.
told told told told told told told told told told told told.
another bomber at the bottom of another lake.

Matsushima in Summertime

loose elastic fastened by dirty knots to threadbare eyepatches.
puttees slipping down like a mummy's buskins.
they come.
on foot or earthward crutch they come.
they the veterans of the defeat.
they come to admire the pine trees that traditionally for the Japanese
    represent permanence.

The Busy

the busy dead.
see.
the busy dead are burying their dead.

Children

hitler's children make pastel sketches in air-cooled rooms in
    northern Europe.
pastoral watercolors in California delicate as the knees of deer.

the children witness.
casualty figures agitate the faces of rapid-fire Teletype printers.

anything goes mercy me.
paper cups are piling up in plastic bags in waste baskets.

the wax reflects computers' flirting lights the red the green.

another reichsmarschall heavy with decorations is checking out of an
    asylum in Sweden today with a clean bill of health of all things.
& a man lays down his life.
he lays it down it is like dropping a name earthward another ace's name
    down.

they took down that honor roll billboard that said lest we forget.

& now rows rows long rows of offspring.
rows of new holes echoing the commanded blanks.
volley echo volley echo volley echo O well well well.

but so what what the hell.
I mean look.
the leopard shark is a cannibal even before it leaves the uterus.